# Leadership Presence

HBR EMOTIONAL INTELLIGENCE SERIES

## HBR Emotional Intelligence Series

The HBR Emotional Intelligence Series features smart, essential reading on the human side of professional life from the pages of *Harvard Business Review*.

*Authentic Leadership*

*Dealing with Difficult People*

*Empathy*

*Happiness*

*Influence and Persuasion*

*Leadership Presence*

*Mindfulness*

*Purpose, Meaning, and Passion*

*Resilience*

Other books on emotional intelligence from *Harvard Business Review*:

*HBR's 10 Must Reads on Emotional Intelligence*

*HBR Guide to Emotional Intelligence*

*HBR Everyday Emotional Intelligence*

# Leadership Presence

HBR EMOTIONAL INTELLIGENCE SERIES

Harvard Business Review Press

Boston, Massachusetts

10 9 8 7 6 5 4 3 2 1

The web addresses referenced in this book were live and correct at the time of the book's publication but may be subject to change.

Library of Congress Cataloging-in-Publication Data

Title: Leadership presence.
Other titles: HBR emotional intelligence series.
Description: Boston, Massachusetts : Harvard Business Review Press, [2018] | Series: HBR emotional intelligence series
Identifiers: LCCN 2017054135 | ISBN  978-1-63369-626-6
Subjects: LCSH: Leadership. | Executive ability. | Emotional intelligence.
Classification: LCC HD57.7 .L4347 2018 | DDC 658.4/092--dc23 LC record available at https://lccn.loc.gov/2017054135

# Contents

# Contents

# Leadership
# Presence

HBR EMOTIONAL INTELLIGENCE SERIES

# 1

# Deconstructing Executive Presence

By John Beeson

I f you ask a group of managers who aspire to the C-suite what it takes to get there, they'll invariably mention executive presence, but they aren't always so clear about what it means. Not too long ago, I conducted a series of off-the-record interviews with senior executives responsible for executive placement in their organizations. I asked them about the "make or break" factors they consider in making C-suite promotion decisions. Executive presence was one of the handful of decision criteria they cited, but even these experienced executives struggled to define what it is and why one person has it and another doesn't. In an increasingly diverse world where senior executives are no longer all six-feet-two-inch males who look like they were sent from central casting, what does it take to create a commanding executive presence? The right clothes? A firm handshake? Those matter, but they don't tell the whole story.

Although executive presence is highly intuitive and difficult to pin down, it ultimately boils down to your ability to project mature self-confidence, a sense that you can take control of difficult, unpredictable situations; make tough decisions in a timely way and hold your own with other talented and strong-willed members of the executive team. If that's the nub of the issue, what style, what behaviors combine to signal that level of self-confidence to others? For some answers, consider three talented managers—two of whom didn't make it to the executive level and one who did.

Every manager would love to have a Frank Simmons on his or her management team. Experienced, results oriented, collaborative, and committed to the company, Frank showed up on succession lists for a number of years, but was never promoted. Although a top performer in his area, Frank always looked a little rumpled and his posture was a bit hunched. When he made presentations to the executive team, he was invariably well prepared, but his lack of comfort was evident in his body language. Normally highly articulate, his presentations were long-winded and rambling. In the Q&A portion of his presentations, he tended to be overly deferential to members of the executive team, and he was hesitant to insert himself into the conversation when the executives got into a debate. As one senior executive said privately, "Frank's an incredible asset to the company, but I just can't envision putting him in front of a customer."

Alicia Wallace was a highly trained marketing manager who had succeeded in every assignment she'd had. However, when it came time to select high-potential people for promotion to more senior levels, she always missed the cut. As much as the senior marketing executives liked and respected her, they were never quite comfortable moving her to the next level. The reason: her apparent disorganization. People would talk about "Alicia being Alicia" when she arrived late to yet another meeting, rushed, harried, and with her files askew. Was this trivial and petty? Perhaps, but on a visceral level, it caused senior people to question her ability to manage a larger staff and maintain the necessary focus on implementing key priorities.

If you entered a room filled with 20 managers, Lydia Taylor, a member of the legal department, wouldn't stand out, but that would change once the dialogue started. Although soft spoken and not terribly aggressive, she was highly respected by her peers as well as the executives with whom she worked. Lydia possessed outstanding listening skills and had an unerring sense of when to enter the conversation to make her point. Unrushed, straightforward, and unflappable, she maintained her calm, even demeanor when others got emotional, and she used her dry sense of humor to defuse difficult situations. When challenged by others, she stood her ground in a firm, nonconfrontational way. Although highly supportive of her internal customers, she was prepared to put her foot down if anyone advocated a position that might put the company at risk. As a result, Lydia was identified as a top candidate and groomed to succeed the company's general counsel.

The age-old question is whether executive presence can be developed? The answer is yes, if you have a baseline of self-confidence and a willingness to deal with the unpredictable situations that go with the territory at the executive level. Start by addressing the basics. Find a couple of trusted people who will give you unvarnished feedback about your dress and grooming and the level of self-confidence you project. As noted, dress and grooming aren't the whole deal, but major problems can create an impediment. One highly talented female manager was privately described by her peers as dressing like a "school marm," while others said a hard-charging manager came off like a "used car salesman." The connotations aren't flattering, nor are they insignificant. People tend not to trust a used car salesman, and school marms aren't typically thought of as creative and risk taking, two qualities central to leading innovation and change at the executive level.

Look for opportunities to hone your presentation skills. Not only is public speaking an important executive requirement, but your ability to "stand and deliver" to an executive group or large audience is frequently viewed as an indicator of your ability to handle pressure. Rehearse a major presentation until you can come off as relaxed and in command, and pay special attention to the Q&A portion since your poise when questioned and ability to think on your feet help you project a sense of self-confidence.

Most important, find your voice as an executive: that is, identify your assets and leverage them to the hilt. Some people are naturally gregarious and can fill a room with their personality. Others, like Lydia Taylor, rely on their listening ability, sense of timing, and ability to maintain their composure when others get emotional. In an increasingly diverse world, executive presence will look very different from one executive to another. However, the constant is building the confidence of others that you can step up as a leader when times get tough.

JOHN BEESON is principal of Beeson Consulting, a management consulting firm specializing in succession planning, executive assessment and coaching, and organization design. He is also the author of *The Unwritten Rules: The Six Skills You Need to Get Promoted to the Executive Level* (Jossey-Bass). Follow him on Twitter @johnrbeeson.

Reprinted from hbr.org, originally published August 22, 2012 (product #H0099M).

2

# How New Managers Can Send the Right Leadership Signals

By Amy Jen Su

One of the most exciting and sometimes anxiety-producing transitions in a career comes when you move from being an individual contributor to becoming a manager. At this juncture, *what you think, what you say, and how you show up*—in effect, your leadership presence—can have a direct impact on those you are now leading and managing for the first time. So, as a new manager, how do you build an authentic and connected leadership presence that has a positive impact on your team and colleagues?

Set a leadership values-based goal. An authentic and connected presence begins from the inside out. How you define the role and what you value will telegraph out to those you work with. As a new manager, spend time to consider the kind of leader you are and hope to be. Set an aspirational goal to serve as a guiding compass. As one new manager shared recently, "my professional leadership goal is to be a genuine and emotionally intelligent manager who inspires others to excellence."

As Ram Charan, Stephen Drotter, and James Noel describe in their book, *The Leadership Pipeline*, "Though this might seem like an easy, natural leadership passage, it's often one where people trip . . . [T]hey make the job transition from individual contribution to manager without making a behavioral or values-based transition . . . They must believe that making time for others, planning, [and] coaching . . . are necessary tasks and their responsibility. More than that, they must view this other-directed work as mission-critical to their success."

Increase your emotional intelligence and situational awareness. As the job now shifts to getting more work done through others, recognize that what motivates or influences you may not be how others are motivated or influenced. In advance of important interactions or meetings, ask yourself:

- Who is the other person or audience?

- What might their perspective on this topic be?

- How are they best motivated or influenced?

- What does the situation at hand call for?

- What are the optimal outcomes and tone?

These questions remind us that leadership presence is not about finding a one-size-fits-all solution. Leadership presence is therefore an "and/both" versus an "either/or." On the one hand, having an effective leadership presence includes being authentic, genuine, and clear on your guiding compass, core values, and convictions. And, on the other hand, it includes being adaptive and agile, demonstrating an ability to connect with different kinds of people through many different communication platforms and technologies.

Be clear and direct, always with respect. As your new role will likely increase your interactions with people of many different styles, having an effective leadership presence includes continually building and practicing the skills of being clear and direct while finding ways of making connections and showing respect. Leadership presence is dynamic and fluid, and encourages a two-way dialogue where we can give authentic voice to our views while staying open to the views and perspectives of others as we work toward a common goal, best outcome, or solution. Here are a few examples of things that can help you cultivate your own voice and listen to the voices of others:

- *Know what you think:* If you are naturally strong at listening and hearing other's opinions, flex your muscles in getting to your own convictions and thoughts more quickly. Before important meetings or interactions, jot down a few bullet points to yourself: *What are the three to five things I believe about this topic or issue?*

- *Ask, listen, and acknowledge:* Conversely, if you are naturally strong at having your own opinions, settle into a greater patience, so that you can make space to hear others. Show you are really listening by asking great questions, clarifying what you've heard, or acknowledging how you're processing the information. In some cases, you might share: *"With this new information, I am experiencing this quite differently. My view has changed."* In other cases, you might end up saying: *"In digesting what you have shared, I am finding I just can't get myself comfortable with that direction. Ultimately, this is coming down to a difference of opinion."*

- *Share the "why":* As a new manager, it's also critical to share the "why" behind your vision, priorities, expectations, feedback, or requests. Don't dilute your message. Instead, make it more powerful by sharing more about the context. Help connect work deliverables or professional development to what's happening at the organizational level. For example, in giving developmental feedback to someone, you could include additional context such as: *"Because the organization is growing so fast, there is opportunity for each member of the team to stretch and step up in the following ways. I'd love to see you take on . . ."* Or, you can strengthen the message by painting the picture of the aspiration: *"I'd love to see us become best in class at this, and here's what will be required."*

Bring a stable and grounded presence in the face of change, stress, or difficult news. The reality is that most of us can exude an effective presence, especially when business is going well or when we are having a good day. As a new manager, however, it's equally important to ask yourself: *What do people experience when I'm stressed out, tired, under deadline, or when someone is bringing me bad news?*

Recognize that what may feel like a passing or fleeting moment of anger, impatience, or hurried insincerity may end up negatively impacting your team and its overall morale and engagement. As author Daniel Goleman writes in his book *Primal Leadership*: "Quite simply, in any human group, the leader has maximal power to sway everyone's emotions . . . [H]ow well leaders manage their moods affects everyone else's moods, which becomes not just a private matter, but a factor in how well a business will do."

Maintaining a stable and grounded presence increases the likelihood that your team will feel comfortable bringing you important information, even if it's bad news, so that you can help to remove obstacles, reset priorities, or get the team back on track. Professor Amy Edmondson's research finds that teams can optimize their learning and performance when there is an environment or culture—most often set by the manager—that promotes both psychological safety and accountability.

To help maintain and sustain a more stable and grounded presence, be sure that you are setting the right priorities for yourself, and that you have strategies for managing the workload of being a leader as you take on this larger role and responsibility as a new manager.

Becoming a new manager is an important leadership passage in your career. Step back and think about your leadership presence and if you are *thinking, saying, and showing up* as you most hope to and intend. Set a values-based leadership goal, increase your emotional intelligence and situational awareness, be direct with respect, and find strategies to maintain and sustain a stable and grounded presence. It's easy in our humbleness to underestimate the impact we have on other's lives as managers.

As professor Clayton Christensen writes in his classic HBR article, "How Will You Measure Your Life?":

*In my mind's eye I saw one of my managers leave for work one morning with a relatively strong level of self-esteem. Then, I pictured her driving home to her family 10 hours later, feeling unappreciated, frustrated, underutilized, and demeaned. I imagined how profoundly her lowered self-esteem affected the way she interacted with her children. The vision in my mind then fast-forwarded to another day, when she drove home with greater self-esteem—feeling that she had learned a lot, had been recognized for achieving valuable things, and had played a significant role in the success of some important initiatives. I then imagined how positively that affected her as a spouse and a parent. My conclusion: Management is the most noble of professions if it's practiced well. No other occupation offers as many ways to help others learn and grow, take responsibility, be recognized for achievement, and contribute to the success of a team.*

AMY JEN SU is a cofounder and managing partner of Paravis Partners, a boutique executive coaching and leadership development firm. She is coauthor, with Muriel Maignan Wilkins, of *Own the Room: Discover Your Signature Voice to Master Your Leadership Presence* (Harvard Business Review Press, 2013). Follow Amy on Twitter @amyjensu.

Reprinted from hbr.org, originally published
August 8, 2017 (product #H03S6X).

# 3

# To Sound Like a Leader, Think About What You Say, and How and When You Say It

By Rebecca Shambaugh

Nancy started her day feeling prepared to brief her executive team on a high-stakes project she had been working on for the past two months. She had rehearsed her slide deck repeatedly, to the point where she had every level of content practically memorized. She arrived at the meeting early and waited patiently, yet anxiously, for her part of the agenda. The meeting began, and within a few minutes Jack, one of the cochairs, asked her to brief the executives on her project and recommendations.

Nancy enthusiastically launched into her presentation, hitting every talking point that she had meticulously rehearsed. With a solid command of the material, she felt at the top of her game and was relieved that she'd spent so much time practicing and preparing for this meeting. But just as she was about to move into her recommendations, Jack interrupted and said, "Nancy, I appreciate your hard work on this project, but it is not relevant to our agenda, and it doesn't have merit for the business objectives we're covering today." Mortified, Nancy retreated to her chair and sat in silence for the rest of the meeting. She couldn't wait to bolt from the room the moment the meeting ended to reflect on how this moment— which she expected would be a positive turning point in her career—had turned into a disaster.

What just happened here? While Nancy was prepared to participate in the meeting, she had failed to think strategically. This common problem trips up many capable managers, executives, and leaders when determining their role in communications, meetings, and other forums. Learning how to develop and convey a more strategic executive voice—in part by understanding context—can help leaders avoid finding themselves, as Nancy did, in a potentially career-damaging situation.

Whether you are an associate manager or a senior executive, what you say, how you say it, when you say it, to whom you say it, and whether you say it in the proper context are critical components for tapping into your full strategic leadership potential. If you want to establish credibility and influence people, particularly when interacting with other executives or senior leadership, it's important to be concise and let individuals know clearly what role you want them to play in the conversation. It's also important to demystify the content of any message you deliver by avoiding jargon and being a person of few—but effective—words.

All of these factors relate to developing a strategic executive voice. Your executive voice is less about your performance; it relates more to your strategic instincts, understanding of context, and awareness of the signals you send in your daily interactions and communications. Like its sister attribute, executive presence, executive voice can seem somewhat intangible and thus difficult to define. But the fact is, we all have a preferred way to communicate with others, and doing this with strategic intent and a solid grasp of context can mean the difference between success and failure in your communication and leadership style.

One of the most important aspects of having an executive voice relates to being a strategic leader. I frequently hear from top executives that they would like to promote one of their high-potential leaders but feel the person is not strategic enough to advance. When I hear managers say this, I try to gently push back and suggest that maybe the problem isn't the candidate's lack of strategic leadership potential; perhaps they are failing to tap into their abilities as a strategic leader.

Whether you have someone on your team who you think lacks strategic readiness or you're worried that *you* might be a leader with untapped strategic potential due to an undeveloped executive voice, read on. Below are some coaching strategies that I use frequently with both male and female executives to help them add a more strategic executive voice to their leadership tool kit.

Understand the context. How often do you find yourself throwing out an unformed idea in a meeting, not speaking up when people are looking for your ideas, or saying something that doesn't quite fit the agenda and suddenly getting that "deer in the headlights" feeling? If these situations sound familiar, what is it that went wrong? In short, these types of tactical errors come down to failing to understand the context of the call, meeting, or discussion that you are in.

For example, if you are the primary authority on a topic, then it's likely that the context would require you to lead the meeting and make any final decisions. But if you are one of several executives who might have input, then sharing your view and connecting the dots with others (rather than stealing the spotlight with your great ideas) would be your role. If you are in learning mode and are not asked to present at a meeting, then your role when it comes to communication would be to observe and listen. Knowing or finding out in advance what your expected role is in a group forum or event can guide you in determining the kind of voice you need for that particular venue and can help ensure that you understand the context before you speak up.

Be a visionary. Sometimes we fail to tap into an executive voice because we focus too much on our own function or role. Strategic leaders are more visionary than that, taking an enterprise view that focuses less on themselves and more on the wider organization. Another part of being visionary is developing the ability to articulate aspirations for the future and a rationale for transformation.

This type of executive vision helps guide decisions around individual and corporate action. You should work toward connecting the dots with your recommendations to show how your decisions affect others around the table, including your staff and the organization as a whole.

Cultivate strategic relationships. One of the best ways to build your strategic thinking is by leveraging relationships more intentionally, with specific business goals in mind. This calls for having senior leaders and executives who bring a strategic perspective of the organization's goals, changes, and top priorities that we may normally not have access to. When you cultivate and invest in broad strategic relationships, it helps you avoid getting caught up in day-to-day minutiae.

It's easy to lose sight of the significance of cultivating new and diverse relationships when you already have a full plate, but part of being able to access a strong executive voice is expanding your knowledge beyond your specific position, department, or area of expertise. To develop your executive voice, take time to reach out to at least one person each week outside of your immediate team or functional area. Try to learn:

- How they fit into the business as a whole

- Their goals and challenges

- Ways you might support them as a strategic business partner

Bring solutions, not just problems. While coaching a wide range of executives, I've seen firsthand that most feel frustrated when people point out challenges but don't offer any resolutions. Leading strategically with a strong executive voice involves problem solving, not just finger-pointing at difficult issues.

You can show up more strategically by doing your homework and taking the lead in analyzing situations. Brainstorm fresh ideas that go beyond the obvious. Even if you don't have the perfect answer, you can demonstrate your ability to come up with clever solutions.

Stay calm in the pressure cooker. People with an effective executive voice aren't easily rattled. Can you provide levelheaded leadership even when—in fact, particularly when—everyone around you is losing their composure? When you can stick with facts instead of getting swept into an emotional tailspin no matter how stressed you feel, you'll be able to lead with a more powerful executive voice.

It can be uncomfortable to recognize and admit personal challenges regarding your executive voice, and at first you may get pushback when making suggestions to improve the executive voice of those on your team. But once you overcome this initial resistance, whether in yourself or others, you'll find it's worth the up-front effort to investigate how to contribute most effectively to important meetings and other communications. By making the necessary adjustments to your approach to participation, you can avoid flying blind and start showing up more strategically in every setting.

REBECCA SHAMBAUGH is an internationally recognized leadership expert, author, and keynote speaker. She's president of SHAMBAUGH, a global leadership development organization, and founder of Women in Leadership and Learning (WILL).

Reprinted from hbr.org, originally published
October 31, 2017 (product #H03ZDX).

# 4

# Connect, Then Lead

By Amy J. C. Cuddy, Matthew Kohut,
and John Neffinger

*s it better to be loved or feared?*

Niccolò Machiavelli pondered that timeless conundrum 500 years ago and hedged his bets. "It may be answered that one should wish to be both," he acknowledged, "but because it is difficult to unite them in one person, it is much safer to be feared than loved."

Now behavioral science is weighing in with research showing that Machiavelli had it partly right. When we judge others—especially our leaders—we look first at two characteristics: how lovable they are (their warmth, communion, or trustworthiness) and how fearsome they are (their strength, agency, or competence). Although there is some disagreement about the proper labels for the traits, researchers agree that they are the two primary dimensions of social judgment.

Why are these traits so important? Because they answer two critical questions: "What are this person's intentions toward me?" and "Is he or she capable of acting on those intentions?" Together, these assessments underlie our emotional and behavioral reactions to other people, groups, and even brands and companies.[1] Research by one of us, Amy Cuddy, and colleagues Susan Fiske of Princeton and Peter Glick of Lawrence University, shows that people judged to be competent but lacking in warmth often elicit envy in others, an emotion involving both respect and resentment that cuts both ways. When we respect someone, we want to cooperate or affiliate ourselves with him or her, but resentment can make that person vulnerable to harsh reprisal (think of disgraced Tyco CEO Dennis Kozlowski, whose extravagance made him an unsympathetic public figure). On the other hand, people judged as warm but incompetent tend to elicit pity, which also involves a mix of emotions: Compassion moves us to help those we pity, but our lack of respect leads us ultimately to neglect them (think of workers who become marginalized as they near retirement or of an employee with outmoded skills in a rapidly evolving industry).

To be sure, we notice plenty of other traits in people, but they're nowhere near as influential as warmth and strength. Indeed, insights from the field of psychology show that these two dimensions account for more than 90% of the variance in our positive or negative impressions we form of the people around us.

So which is better, being lovable or being strong? Most leaders today tend to emphasize their strength, competence, and credentials in the workplace, but that is exactly the wrong approach. Leaders who project strength before establishing trust run the risk of eliciting fear, and along with it, a host of dysfunctional behaviors. Fear can undermine cognitive potential, creativity, and problem solving, and cause employees to get stuck and even disengage. It's a "hot" emotion, with long-lasting effects. It burns into our memory in a way that cooler emotions don't. Research by Jack Zenger and Joseph Folkman drives this point home: In a study of 51,836 leaders, only 27 of them were rated in the bottom quartile in terms of likability and in the top quartile in terms of overall leadership effectiveness—in other words, the chances that a manager who is strongly disliked will be considered a good leader are only about one in 2,000.

A growing body of research suggests that the way to influence—and to lead—is to begin with warmth. Warmth is the conduit of influence: It facilitates trust and the communication and absorption of ideas. Even a few small nonverbal signals—a nod, a smile, an open gesture—can show people that you're pleased to be in their company and attentive to their concerns. Prioritizing warmth helps you connect immediately with those around you, demonstrating that you hear them, understand them, and can be trusted by them.

## When strength comes first

Most of us work hard to demonstrate our competence. We want to see ourselves as strong—and want others to see us the same way. We focus on warding off challenges to our strength and providing abundant evidence of competence. We feel compelled to demonstrate that we're up to the job, by striving to present the most innovative ideas in meetings, being the first to tackle a challenge, and working the longest hours. We're sure of our own intentions and thus don't feel the need to prove that we're trustworthy, despite the fact that evidence of trustworthiness is the first thing we look for in others.

Organizational psychologists Andrea Abele of the University of Erlangen-Nuremberg and Bogdan Wojciszke of the University of Gdańsk have documented this phenomenon across a variety of settings. In one experiment, when asked to choose between training programs focusing on competence-related skills (such as time management) and warmth-related ones (providing social support, for instance), most participants opted for competence-based training for themselves but soft-skills training for others. In another experiment, in which participants were asked to describe an event that shaped their self-image, most told stories about themselves that emphasized their own competence and self-determination ("I passed my pilot's license test on the first try"), whereas when they described a similar event for someone else, they focused on that person's warmth and generosity ("My friend tutored his neighbor's child in math and refused to accept any payment").

But putting competence first undermines leadership: Without a foundation of trust, people in the organization may comply outwardly with a leader's wishes, but they're much less likely to conform privately—to adopt the values, culture, and mission of the organization in a sincere, lasting way. Workplaces lacking in trust often have a culture of "every employee for himself," in which people feel that they must be vigilant about protecting their interests. Employees can become reluctant to help others because they're unsure of whether their efforts will be reciprocated or recognized. The result: Shared organizational resources fall victim to the tragedy of the commons.

## When warmth comes first

Although most of us strive to demonstrate our strength, warmth contributes significantly more to others' evaluations of us, and it's judged before competence. Princeton social psychologist Alex Todorov and colleagues study the cognitive and neural mechanisms that drive our "spontaneous trait inferences"—

the snap judgments we make when briefly looking at faces. Their research shows that when making those judgments, people consistently pick up on warmth faster than on competence. This preference for warmth holds true in other areas as well. In a study led by Oscar Ybarra of the University of Michigan, participants playing a word game identified warmth-related words (such as "friendly") significantly faster than competence-related ones (such as "skillful").

Behavioral economists, for their part, have shown that judgments of trustworthiness generally lead to significantly higher economic gains. For example, Mascha van 't Wout of Brown University and Alan Sanfey of the University of Arizona asked subjects to determine how an endowment should be allocated. Players invested more money, with no guarantee of return, in partners whom they perceived to be more trustworthy on the basis of a glance at their faces.[2]

In management settings, trust increases information sharing, openness, fluidity, and cooperation. If coworkers can be trusted to do the right thing and live up to their commitments, planning, coordination, and execution are much easier. Trust also facilitates the exchange and acceptance of ideas—it allows people to hear others' messages—and boosts the quantity and quality of the ideas that are produced within an organization. Most important, trust provides the opportunity to change people's attitudes and beliefs, not just their outward behavior. That's the sweet spot when it comes to influence and the ability to get people to fully accept your message.

## The happy warrior

The best way to gain influence is to combine warmth and strength—as difficult as Machiavelli says that may be to do. The traits can actually be mutually reinforcing: Feeling a sense of personal strength

## HOW WILL PEOPLE REACT TO YOUR STYLE?

Research by Amy Cuddy, Susan Fiske, and Peter Glick suggests that the way others perceive your levels of warmth and competence determines the emotions you'll elicit and your ability to influence a situation. For example, if you're highly competent but show only moderate warmth, you'll get people to go along with you, but you won't earn their true engagement and support. And if you show no warmth, beware of those who may try to derail your efforts—and maybe your career.

helps us to be more open, less threatened, and less threatening in stressful situations. When we feel confident and calm, we project authenticity and warmth.

Understanding a little bit about our chemical makeup can shed some light on how this works. The

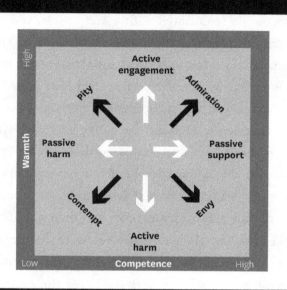

neuropeptides oxytocin and arginine vasopressin, for instance, have been linked to our ability to form human attachments, to feel and express warmth, and to behave altruistically. Recent research also suggests that, across the animal kingdom, feelings of strength and power have close ties to two hormones: testosterone (associated with assertiveness, reduced fear, and willingness to compete and take risks) and cortisol (associated with stress and stress reactivity).

One study, by Jennifer Lerner, Gary Sherman, Amy Cuddy, and colleagues, brought hundreds of people participating in Harvard executive-education programs into the lab and compared their levels of cortisol with the average levels of the general population. The leaders reported less stress and anxiety than did the general population, and their physiology backed that up: Their cortisol levels were significantly lower. Moreover, the higher their rank and the more subordinates they managed, the lower their cortisol levels. Why? Most likely because the leaders had a heightened sense of control—a psychological factor known to have a powerful stress-buffering effect. According to research by Pranjal Mehta of the University of Oregon and Robert Josephs of the University of Texas, the most effective leaders, regardless of gender, have a unique physiological profile, with relatively high testosterone and relatively low cortisol.

Such leaders face troubles without being troubled. Their behavior is not relaxed, but they are relaxed emotionally. They're often viewed as "happy warriors," and the effect of their demeanor on those around them is compelling. Happy warriors reassure us that whatever challenges we may face, things will work out in the end. Ann Richards, the former governor of Texas, played the happy warrior by pairing her assertiveness and authority with a big smile and a quick wit that made it clear she did not let the rough-and-tumble world of politics get her down.

During crises, these are the people who are able to keep that influence conduit open and may even expand it. Most people hate uncertainty, but they tolerate it much better when they can look to a leader who they believe has their back and is calm, clearheaded, and courageous. These are the people we trust. These are the people we listen to.

There are physical exercises that can help to summon self-confidence—and even alter your body's chemistry to be more like that of a happy warrior. Dana Carney, Amy Cuddy, and Andy Yap suggest that people adopt "power poses" associated with dominance and strength across the animal kingdom. These postures are open, expansive, and space-occupying (imagine Wonder Woman and Superman standing tall with their hands on their hips and feet spread apart). By adopting these postures for just two minutes before social encounters, their research shows, participants significantly increased their testosterone and decreased their cortisol levels.

Bear in mind that the signals we send can be ambiguous—we can see someone's reaction to our presence, but we may not be sure exactly what the person is reacting to. We may feel a leader's warmth but remain unsure whether it is directed at us; we sense her strength but need reassurance that it is squarely aimed at the shared challenge we face. And, as we noted earlier, judgments are often made quickly, on the basis of nonverbal cues. Especially when facing a high-pressure situation, it is useful for leaders to go through a brief warm-up routine beforehand to get in the right state of mind, practicing and adopting an attitude that will help them project positive nonverbal signals. We refer to this approach as "inside out," in contrast to the "outside-in" strategy of trying to consciously execute specific nonverbal behaviors in the moment. Think of the difference between method acting and classical acting: In method acting, the actor experiences the emotions of the character and naturally produces an authentic performance, whereas in classical acting, actors learn to exercise precise control of their nonverbal signals. Generally speaking, an inside-out approach is more effective.

There are many tactics for projecting warmth and competence, and these can be dialed up or down as needed. Two of us, John Neffinger and Matt Kohut, work with leaders from many walks of life in mastering both nonverbal and verbal cues. Let's look now at some best practices.

51

## WHY WARMTH TRUMPS STRENGTH

The primacy of warmth manifests in many interrelated ways that powerfully underscore the importance of connecting with people before trying to lead them.

### The Need to Affiliate

People have a need to be included, to feel a sense of belonging. In fact, some psychologists would argue that the drive to affiliate ranks among our primary needs as humans. Experiments by neuroscientist Naomi Eisenberger and colleagues suggest that the need is so strong that when we are ostracized—even by virtual strangers—we experience pain that is akin to strong physical pain.

## "Us" Versus "Them"

In recent decades, few areas have received as much attention from social psychology researchers as group dynamics, and for good reason: The preference for the groups to which one belongs is so strong that even under extreme conditions—such as knowing that membership in a group was randomly assigned and that the groups themselves are arbitrary— people consistently prefer fellow group members to nonmembers. As a leader, you must make sure you're a part of the key groups in your organization. In fact, you want to be the aspirational member of the group, the chosen representative of the group. As soon as you become one of "them"—the management, the leadership—you begin to lose people.

*(Continued)*

## WHY WARMTH TRUMPS STRENGTH

### The Desire to Be Understood

People deeply desire to be heard and seen. Sadly, as important as perspective taking is to good leadership, being in a position of power decreases people's understanding of others' points of view. When we have power over others, our ability to see them as individuals diminishes. So leaders need to consciously and consistently make the effort to imagine walking in the shoes of the people they are leading.

# How to project warmth

Efforts to appear warm and trustworthy by consciously controlling your nonverbal signals can backfire: All too often, you'll come off as wooden and inauthentic instead. Here are ways to avoid that trap.

## *Find the right level*

When people want to project warmth, they sometimes amp up the enthusiasm in their voice, increasing their volume and dynamic range to convey delight. That can be effective in the right setting, but if those around you have done nothing in particular to earn your adulation, they'll assume either that you're faking it or that you fawn over everyone indiscriminately.

A better way to create vocal warmth is to speak with lower pitch and volume, as you would if you were comforting a friend. Aim for a tone that suggests that you're leveling with people—that you're sharing the straight scoop, with no pretense or emotional adornment. In doing so, you signal that you trust those you're talking with to handle things the right way. You might even occasionally share a personal story—one that feels private but not inappropriate—in a confiding tone of voice to demonstrate that you're being forthcoming and open. Suppose, for instance, that you want to establish a bond with new employees you're meeting for the first time. You might offer something personal right off the bat, such as recalling how you felt at a similar point in your career. That's often enough to set a congenial tone.

## Validate feelings

Before people decide what they think of your message, they decide what they think of *you*. If you show your employees that you hold roughly the same worldview they do, you demonstrate not only empathy but, in their eyes, common sense—the ultimate qualification for being listened to. So if you want colleagues to listen and agree with you, first agree with them.

Imagine, for instance, that your company is undergoing a major reorganization and your group is feeling deep anxiety over what the change could mean—for quality, innovation, job security. Acknowledge people's fear and concerns when you speak to them, whether in formal meetings or during water-cooler chats. Look them in the eye and say, "I know everybody's feeling a lot of uncertainty right now, and it's unsettling." People will respect you for addressing the elephant in the room, and will be more open to hearing what you have to say.

## ARE YOU PROJECTING WARMTH?

How you present yourself in workplace settings matters a great deal to how you're perceived by others. Even if you're not feeling particularly warm, practicing these approaches and using them in formal and informal situations can help clear your path to influence.

*(Continued)*

## ARE YOU PROJECTING WARMTH?

**Warm**

- When standing, balance your weight primarily on one hip to avoid appearing rigid or tense.
- Tilt your head slightly and keep your hands open and welcoming.

**Cold**

- Avoid standing with your chin pointed down.
- Don't pivot your body away from the person you're engaging with.
- Avoid closed-hand positions and cutting motions.

*(Continued)*

## ARE YOU PROJECTING WARMTH?

**Warm**

- Lean inward in a nonaggressive manner to signal interest and engagement.
- Place your hands comfortably on your knees or rest them on the table.
- Aim for body language that feels professional but relaxed.

### Cold

- Try not to angle your body away from the person you're engaging.
- Crossing your arms indicates coldness and a lack of receptivity.
- Avoid sitting "at attention" or in an aggressive posture.

Illustration: Colin Hayes

## *Smile—and mean it*

When we smile sincerely, the warmth becomes self-reinforcing: Feeling happy makes us smile, and smiling makes us happy. This facial feedback is also contagious. We tend to mirror one another's nonverbal expressions and emotions, so when we see someone beaming and emanating genuine warmth, we can't resist smiling ourselves.

Warmth is not easy to fake, of course, and a polite smile fools no one. To project warmth, you have to genuinely feel it. A natural smile, for instance, involves not only the muscles around the mouth but also those around the eyes—the crow's feet.

So how do you produce a natural smile? Find some reason to feel happy wherever you may be, even if you have to resort to laughing at your predicament. Introverts in social settings can single out one person to focus on. This can help you channel the sense of comfort you feel with close friends or family.

For example, KNP Communications worked with a manager who was having trouble connecting with her employees. Having come up through the ranks as a highly analytic engineer, she projected competence and determination, but not much warmth. We noticed, however, that when she talked about where she grew up and what she learned about life from the tight-knit community in her neighborhood, her demeanor relaxed and she smiled broadly. By including a brief anecdote about her upbringing when she kicked off a meeting or made a presentation, she was able to show her colleagues a warm and relatable side of herself.

One thing to avoid: smiling with your eyebrows raised at anyone over the age of five. This suggests that you are overly eager to please and be liked. It also signals anxiety, which, like warmth, is contagious. It will cost you much more in strength than you will gain in warmth.

# How to project strength

Strength or competence can be established by virtue of the position you hold, your reputation, and your actual performance. But your presence, or demeanor, always counts, too. The way you carry yourself doesn't establish your skill level, of course, but it is taken as strong evidence of your attitude—how serious you are and how determined to tackle a challenge—and that is an important component of overall strength. The trick is to cultivate a demeanor of strength without seeming menacing.

## *Feel in command*

Warmth may be harder to fake, but confidence is harder to talk yourself into. Feeling like an impostor— that you don't belong in the position you're in and are going to be "found out"—is very common. But self-doubt completely undermines your ability to project confidence, enthusiasm, and passion, the qualities that make up presence. In fact, if you see yourself as an impostor, others will, too. Feeling in command and confident is about connecting with yourself. And when we are connected with ourselves, it is much easier to connect with others.

Holding your body in certain ways, as we discussed previously, can help. Although we refer to these postures as power poses, they don't increase your dominance over others. They're about personal power—your agency and ability to self-regulate. Recent research led by Dacher Keltner of the University of California, Berkeley, shows that feeling powerful in this way allows you to shed the fears and inhibitions that can prevent you from bringing your fullest, most authentic and enthusiastic self to a high-stakes professional situation, such as a pitch to investors or a speech to an influential audience.

## *Stand up straight*

It is hard to overstate the importance of good posture in projecting authority and an intention to be taken seriously. As Maya Angelou wrote, "Stand up straight and realize who you are, that you tower over your circumstances." Good posture does not mean the exaggerated chest-out pose known in the military as standing at attention, or raising one's chin up high. It just means reaching your full height, using your muscles to straighten the S-curve in your spine rather than slouching. It sounds trivial, but maximizing the physical space your body takes up makes a substantial difference in how your audience reacts to you, regardless of your height.

## *Get ahold of yourself*

When you move, move deliberately and precisely to a specific spot rather than casting your limbs about loose-jointedly. And when you are finished moving, be still. Twitching, fidgeting, or other visual static sends the signal that you're not in control. Stillness demonstrates calm. Combine that with good posture, and you'll achieve what's known as poise, which telegraphs equilibrium and stability, important aspects of credible leadership presence.

Standing tall is an especially good way to project strength because it doesn't interfere with warmth in the way that other signals of strength—cutting gestures, a furrowed brow, an elevated chin—often do. People who instruct their children to stand up straight and smile are on to something: This simple combination is perhaps the best way to project strength and warmth simultaneously. If you want to effectively lead others, you have to get the warmth-competence dynamic right. Projecting both traits at once is difficult, but the two can be mutually reinforcing—and the rewards substantial. Earning the trust and appreciation of those around you feels good. Feeling in command of a situation does, too. Doing both lets you influence people more effectively.

The strategies we suggest may seem awkward at first, but they will soon create a positive feedback loop. Being calm and confident creates space to be warm, open, and appreciative, to choose to act in ways that reflect and express your values and priorities. Once you establish your warmth, your strength is received as a welcome reassurance. Your leadership becomes not a threat but a gift.

AMY J. C. CUDDY is a former associate professor of business administration at Harvard Business School. MATTHEW KOHUT and JOHN NEFFINGER are the authors of *Compelling People: The Hidden Qualities That Make Us Influential* (Hudson Street Press, 2013) and principals at KNP Communications.

## Notes

1. A. J. C. Cuddy, P. Glick, and A. Beninger, "The Dynamics of Warmth and Competence Judgments, and Their

Outcomes in Organizations," *Research in Organizational Behavior* 31 (2011): 73–98.

2. M. van 't Wout and A. G. Sanfey, "Friend or Foe: The Effect of Implicit Trustworthiness Judgments in Social Decision-Making," *Cognition* 108, no. 3 (2008): 796–803.

Reprinted from *Harvard Business Review*,
July–August 2013 (product #R1307C).

# 5

# The Power of Talk: Who Gets Heard and Why

By Deborah Tannen

The head of a large division of a multinational corporation was running a meeting devoted to performance assessment. Each senior manager stood up, reviewed the individuals in his group, and evaluated them for promotion. Although there were women in every group, not one of them made the cut. One after another, each manager declared, in effect, that every woman in his group didn't have the self-confidence needed to be promoted. The division head began to doubt his ears. How could it be that all the talented women in the division suffered from a lack of self-confidence?

In all likelihood, they didn't. Consider the many women who have left large corporations to start their own businesses, obviously exhibiting enough confidence to succeed on their own. Judgments about confidence can be inferred only from the way people present themselves, and much of that presentation is in the form of talk.

The CEO of a major corporation told me that he often has to make decisions in five minutes about matters on which others may have worked five months. He said he uses this rule: If the person making the proposal seems confident, the CEO approves it. If not, he says no. This might seem like a reasonable approach. But my field of research, socio-linguistics, suggests otherwise. The CEO obviously thinks he knows what a confident person sounds like. But his judgment, which may be dead right for some people, may be dead wrong for others.

Communication isn't as simple as saying what you mean. How you say what you mean is crucial, and differs from one person to the next, because using language is learned social behavior: How we talk and listen are deeply influenced by cultural experience. Although we might think that our ways of saying what we mean are natural, we can run into trouble if we interpret and evaluate others as if they necessarily felt the same way we'd feel if we spoke the way they did.

Since 1974, I have been researching the influence of linguistic style on conversations and human relationships. In the past four years, I have extended that research to the workplace, where I have observed how ways of speaking learned in childhood affect judgments of competence and confidence, as well as who gets heard, who gets credit, and what gets done.

The division head who was dumbfounded to hear that all the talented women in his organization lacked confidence was probably right to be skeptical. The senior managers were judging the women in their groups by their own linguistic norms, but women—like people who have grown up in a different culture—have often learned different styles of speaking than men, which can make them seem less competent and self-assured than they are.

## What is linguistic style?

Everything that is said must be said in a certain way—in a certain tone of voice, at a certain rate of speed, and with a certain degree of loudness. Whereas often we consciously consider what to say before speaking, we rarely think about how to say it, unless the situation is obviously loaded—for example, a job interview or a tricky performance review. Linguistic style refers to a person's characteristic speaking pattern. It includes such features as directness or indirectness, pacing and pausing, word choice, and the use of such elements as jokes, figures of speech, stories, questions, and apologies. In other words, linguistic style is a set of culturally learned signals by which we not only communicate what we mean but also interpret others' meaning and evaluate one another as people.

Consider turn taking, one element of linguistic style. Conversation is an enterprise in which people take turns: One person speaks, then the other responds. However, this apparently simple exchange requires a subtle negotiation of signals so that you know when the other person is finished and it's your turn to begin. Cultural factors such as country or region of origin and ethnic background influence how long a pause seems natural. When Bob, who is from Detroit, has a conversation with his colleague Joe, from New York City, it's hard for him to get a word in edgewise because he expects a slightly longer pause between turns than Joe does. A pause of that length never comes because, before it has a chance to, Joe senses an uncomfortable silence, which he fills with more talk of his own. Both men fail to realize that differences in conversational style are getting in their way. Bob thinks that Joe is pushy and uninterested in what he has to say, and Joe thinks that Bob doesn't have much to contribute. Similarly, when Sally relocated from Texas to Washington, D.C., she kept searching for the right time to break in during staff meetings—and never found it. Although in Texas she was considered outgoing and confident, in Washington she was perceived as shy and retiring. Her boss even suggested she take an assertiveness training course. Thus, slight differences in conversational style—in these cases, a few seconds of pause—can have a surprising impact on who gets heard and on the judgments, including psychological ones, that are made about people and their abilities.

Every utterance functions on two levels. We're all familiar with the first one: Language communicates ideas. The second level is mostly invisible to us, but it plays a powerful role in communication. As a form of social behavior, language also negotiates relationships. Through ways of speaking, we signal—and create—the relative status of speakers and their level of rapport. If you say, "Sit down!" you are signaling that you have higher status than the person you are addressing, that you are so close to each other that you can drop all pleasantries, or that you are angry. If you say, "I would be honored if you would sit down," you are signaling great respect—or great sarcasm, depending on your tone of voice, the situation, and what you both know about how close you really are. If you say, "You must be so tired. Why don't you sit down," you are communicating either closeness and concern or condescension. Each of these ways of saying "the same thing"—telling someone to sit down—can have a vastly different meaning.

In every community known to linguists, the patterns that constitute linguistic style are relatively different for men and women. What's "natural" for most men speaking a given language is, in some cases, different from what's "natural" for most women. That is because we learn ways of speaking as children growing up, especially from peers, and children tend to play with other children of the same sex. The research of sociologists, anthropologists, and psychologists observing American children at play has shown that, although both girls and boys find ways of creating rapport and negotiating status, girls tend to learn conversational rituals that focus on the rapport dimension of relationships whereas boys tend to learn rituals that focus on the status dimension.

Girls tend to play with a single best friend or in small groups, and they spend a lot of time talking. They use language to negotiate how close they are; for example, the girl you tell your secrets to becomes your best friend. Girls learn to downplay ways in which one is better than the others and to emphasize ways in which they are all the same. From childhood, most girls learn that sounding too sure of themselves will make them unpopular with their peers—although nobody really takes such modesty literally. A group of girls will ostracize a girl who calls attention to her own superiority and criticize her by saying, "She thinks she's something"; and a girl who tells others what to do is called "bossy." Thus, girls learn to talk in ways that balance their own needs with those of others—to save face for one another in the broadest sense of the term.

Boys tend to play very differently. They usually play in larger groups in which more boys can be included, but not everyone is treated as an equal. Boys with high status in their group are expected to emphasize rather than downplay their status, and usually one or several boys will be seen as the leader or leaders. Boys generally don't accuse one another of being bossy, because the leader is expected to tell lower-status boys what to do. Boys learn to use language to negotiate their status in the group by displaying their abilities and knowledge, and by challenging others and resisting challenges. Giving orders is one way of getting and keeping the high-status role. Another is taking center stage by telling stories or jokes.

This is not to say that all boys and girls grow up this way or feel comfortable in these groups or are equally successful at negotiating within these norms. But, for the most part, these childhood play groups are where boys and girls learn their conversational styles. In this sense, they grow up in different worlds. The result is that women and men tend to have different habitual ways of saying what they mean, and conversations between them can be like cross-cultural communication: You can't assume that the other person means what you would mean if you said the same thing in the same way.

My research in companies across the United States shows that the lessons learned in childhood carry over into the workplace. Consider the following example: A focus group was organized at a major multinational company to evaluate a recently implemented flextime policy. The participants sat in a circle and discussed the new system. The group concluded that it was excellent, but they also agreed on ways to improve it. The meeting went well and was deemed a success by all, according to my own observations and everyone's comments to me. But the next day, I was in for a surprise.

I had left the meeting with the impression that Phil had been responsible for most of the suggestions adopted by the group. But as I typed up my notes, I noticed that Cheryl had made almost all those suggestions. I had thought that the key ideas came from Phil because he had picked up Cheryl's points and supported them, speaking at greater length in doing so than she had in raising them.

It would be easy to regard Phil as having stolen Cheryl's ideas—and her thunder. But that would be inaccurate. Phil never claimed Cheryl's ideas as his own. Cheryl herself told me later that she left the meeting confident she had contributed significantly, and that she appreciated Phil's support. She volunteered, with a laugh, "It was not one of those times when a woman says something and it's ignored, then a man says it and it's picked up." In other words, Cheryl and Phil worked well as a team, the group fulfilled its charge, and the company got what it needed. So what was the problem?

I went back and asked all the participants who they thought had been the most influential group member, the one most responsible for the ideas that had been adopted. The pattern of answers was revealing. The two other women in the group named Cheryl. Two of the three men named Phil. Of the men, only Phil named Cheryl. In other words, in this instance, the women evaluated the contribution of another woman more accurately than the men did.

Meetings like this take place daily in companies around the country. Unless managers are unusually good at listening closely to how people say what they mean, the talents of someone like Cheryl may well be undervalued and underutilized.

## One up, one down

Individual speakers vary in how sensitive they are to the social dynamics of language—in other words, to the subtle nuances of what others say to them. Men tend to be sensitive to the power dynamics of interaction, speaking in ways that position themselves as one up and resisting being put in a one-down position by others. Women tend to react more strongly to the rapport dynamic, speaking in ways that save face for others and buffering statements that could be seen as putting others in a one-down position. These linguistic patterns are pervasive; you can hear them in hundreds of exchanges in the workplace every day. And, as in the case of Cheryl and Phil, they affect who gets heard and who gets credit.

## Getting credit

Even so small a linguistic strategy as the choice of pronoun can affect who gets credit. In my research in the workplace, I heard men say "I" in situations where I heard women say "we." For example, one publishing company executive said, "I'm hiring a new manager. I'm going to put him in charge of my marketing division," as if he owned the corporation. In stark contrast, I recorded women saying "we" when referring to work they alone had done. One woman explained that it would sound too self-promoting to claim credit in an obvious way by saying, "I did this." Yet she expected—sometimes vainly—that others would know it was her work and would give her the credit she did not claim for herself.

Managers might leap to the conclusion that women who do not take credit for what they've done should be taught to do so. But that solution is problematic because we associate ways of speaking with moral qualities: The way we speak is who we are and who we want to be.

Veronica, a senior researcher in a high-tech company, had an observant boss. He noticed that many of the ideas coming out of the group were hers but that often someone else trumpeted them around the office and got credit for them. He advised her to "own" her ideas and make sure she got the credit. But Veronica found she simply didn't enjoy her work if she had to approach it as what seemed to her an unattractive and unappealing "grabbing game." It was her dislike of such behavior that had led her to avoid it in the first place.

Whatever the motivation, women are less likely than men to have learned to blow their own horn. And they are more likely than men to believe that if they do so, they won't be liked.

Many have argued that the growing trend of assigning work to teams may be especially congenial to women, but it may also create complications for performance evaluation. When ideas are generated and work is accomplished in the privacy of the team, the outcome of the team's effort may become associated with the person most vocal about reporting results. There are many women and men—but probably relatively more women—who are reluctant to put themselves forward in this way and who consequently risk not getting credit for their contributions.

## Confidence and boasting

The CEO who based his decisions on the confidence level of speakers was articulating a value that is widely shared in U.S. businesses: One way to judge confidence is by an individual's behavior, especially verbal behavior. Here again, many women are at a disadvantage.

Studies show that women are more likely to downplay their certainty and men are more likely to minimize their doubts. Psychologist Laurie Heatherington and her colleagues devised an ingenious experiment, which they reported in the journal *Sex Roles*.[1] They asked hundreds of incoming college students to predict what grades they would get in their first year.

Some subjects were asked to make their predictions privately by writing them down and placing them in an envelope; others were asked to make their predictions publicly, in the presence of a researcher. The results showed that more women than men predicted lower grades for themselves if they made their predictions publicly. If they made their predictions privately, the predictions were the same as those of the men—and the same as their actual grades. This study provides evidence that what comes across as lack of confidence—predicting lower grades for oneself—may reflect not one's actual level of confidence but the desire not to seem boastful.

These habits with regard to appearing humble or confident result from the socialization of boys and girls by their peers in childhood play. As adults, both women and men find these behaviors reinforced by the positive responses they get from friends and relatives who share the same norms. But the norms of behavior in the U.S. business world are based on the style of interaction that is more common among men—at least, among American men.

## Asking questions

Although asking the right questions is one of the hallmarks of a good manager, how and when questions are asked can send unintended signals about competence and power. In a group, if only one person asks questions, he or she risks being seen as the only ignorant one. Furthermore, we judge others not only by how they speak but also by how they are spoken to. The person who asks questions may end up being lectured to and looking like a novice under a schoolmaster's tutelage. The way boys are socialized makes them more likely to be aware of the underlying power dynamic by which a question asker can be seen in a one-down position.

One practicing physician learned the hard way that any exchange of information can become the basis for judgments—or misjudgments—about competence. During her training, she received a negative evaluation that she thought was unfair, so she asked her supervising physician for an explanation. He said that she knew less than her peers. Amazed at his answer, she asked how he had reached that conclusion. He said, "You ask more questions."

Along with cultural influences and individual personality, gender seems to play a role in whether and when people ask questions. For example, of all the observations I've made in lectures and books, the one that sparks the most enthusiastic flash of recognition is that men are less likely than women to stop and ask for directions when they are lost. I explain that men often resist asking for directions because they are aware that it puts them in a one-down position and because they value the independence that comes with finding their way by themselves. Asking for directions while driving is only one instance—along with many others that researchers have examined—

in which men seem less likely than women to ask questions. I believe this is because they are more attuned than women to the potential face-losing aspect of asking questions. And men who believe that asking questions might reflect negatively on them may, in turn, be likely to form a negative opinion of others who ask questions in situations where they would not.

## Conversational rituals

Conversation is fundamentally ritual in the sense that we speak in ways our culture has conventionalized and expect certain types of responses. Take greetings, for example. I have heard visitors to the United States complain that Americans are hypocritical because they ask how you are but aren't interested in the answer. To Americans, "How are you?" is obviously a ritualized way to start a conversation rather than a literal request for information. In other parts of the world, including the Philippines, people ask each other, "Where are you going?" when they meet. The question seems intrusive to Americans, who do not realize that it, too, is a ritual query to which the only expected reply is a vague "Over there."

It's easy and entertaining to observe different rituals in foreign countries. But we don't expect differences, and are far less likely to recognize the ritualized nature of our conversations, when we are with our compatriots at work. Our differing rituals can be even more problematic when we think we're all speaking the same language.

## Apologies

Consider the simple phrase *I'm sorry*.

*Catherine:* How did that big presentation go?

*Bob:* Oh, not very well. I got a lot of flak from the VP for finance, and I didn't have the numbers at my fingertips.

*Catherine:* Oh, I'm sorry. I know how hard you worked on that.

In this case, *I'm sorry* probably means "I'm sorry that happened," not "I apologize," unless it was Catherine's responsibility to supply Bob with the numbers for the presentation. Women tend to say *I'm sorry* more frequently than men—and often they intend it in this way—as a ritualized means of expressing concern. It's one of many learned elements of conversational style that girls often use to establish rapport. Ritual apologies—like other conversational rituals—work well when both parties share the same assumptions about their use. But people who utter frequent ritual apologies may end up appearing weaker, less confident, and literally more blameworthy than people who don't.

Apologies tend to be regarded differently by men, who are more likely to focus on the status implications of exchanges. Many men avoid apologies because they see them as putting the speaker in a one-down position. I observed with some amazement an encounter among several lawyers engaged in a negotiation over a speakerphone. At one point, the lawyer in whose office I was sitting accidentally elbowed the telephone and cut off the call. When his secretary got the parties back on again, I expected him to say what I would have said: "Sorry about that. I knocked the phone with my elbow." Instead, he said, "Hey, what happened? One minute you were there; the next minute you were gone!" This lawyer seemed to have an automatic impulse not to admit fault if he didn't have to. For me, it was one of those pivotal moments when you realize that the world you live in is not the one everyone lives in and that the way you assume is the way to talk is really only one of many.

Those who caution managers not to undermine their authority by apologizing are approaching interaction from the perspective of the power dynamic. In many cases, this strategy is effective. On the other hand, when I asked people what frustrated them in their jobs, one frequently voiced complaint was working with or for someone who refuses to apologize or admit fault. In other words, accepting responsibility for errors and admitting mistakes may be an equally effective or superior strategy in some settings.

## Feedback

Styles of giving feedback contain a ritual element that often is the cause for misunderstanding. Consider the following exchange: A manager had to tell her marketing director to rewrite a report. She began this potentially awkward task by citing the report's strengths and then moved to the main point: the weaknesses that needed to be remedied. The marketing director seemed to understand and accept his supervisor's comments, but his revision contained only minor changes and failed to address the major weaknesses. When the manager told him of her dissatisfaction, he accused her of misleading him: "You told me it was fine."

The impasse resulted from different linguistic styles. To the manager, it was natural to buffer the criticism by beginning with praise. Telling her subordinate that his report is inadequate and has to be rewritten puts him in a one-down position. Praising him for the parts that are good is a ritualized way of saving face for him. But the marketing director did not share his supervisor's assumption about how feedback should be given. Instead, he assumed that what she mentioned first was the main point and that what she brought up later was an afterthought.

Those who expect feedback to come in the way the manager presented it would appreciate her tact and would regard a more blunt approach as unnecessarily callous. But those who share the marketing director's assumptions would regard the blunt approach as honest and no-nonsense, and the manager's as obfuscating. Because each one's assumptions seemed self-evident, each blamed the other: The manager thought the marketing director was not listening, and he thought she had not communicated clearly or had changed her mind. This is significant because it illustrates that incidents labeled vaguely as "poor communication" may be the result of differing linguistic styles.

## Compliments

Exchanging compliments is a common ritual, especially among women. A mismatch in expectations about this ritual left Susan, a manager in the human resources field, in a one-down position. She and her colleague Bill had both given presentations at a national conference. On the airplane home, Susan told Bill, "That was a great talk!" "Thank you," he said. Then she asked, "What did you think of mine?" He responded with a lengthy and detailed critique, as she listened uncomfortably. An unpleasant feeling of having been put down came over her. Somehow she had been positioned as the novice in need of his expert advice. Even worse, she had only herself to blame, since she had, after all, asked Bill what he thought of her talk.

But had Susan asked for the response she received? When she asked Bill what he thought about her talk, she expected to hear not a critique but a compliment. In fact, her question had been an attempt to repair a ritual gone awry. Susan's initial compliment to Bill was the kind of automatic recognition she felt was more or less required after a colleague gives a presentation, and she expected Bill to respond with a matching compliment. She was just talking automatically, but he either sincerely misunderstood the ritual or simply took the opportunity to bask in the one-up position of critic. Whatever his motivation, it was Susan's attempt to spark an exchange of compliments that gave him an opening.

Although this exchange could have occurred between two men, it does not seem coincidental that it happened between a man and a woman. Linguist

Janet Holmes discovered that women pay more compliments than men.[2] And, as I have observed, fewer men are likely to ask, "What did you think of my talk?" precisely because the question might invite an unwanted critique.

In the social structure of the peer groups in which they grow up, boys are indeed looking for opportunities to put others down and take the one-up position for themselves. In contrast, one of the rituals girls learn is taking the one-down position but assuming that the other person will recognize the ritual nature of the self-denigration and pull them back up.

The exchange between Susan and Bill also suggests how women's and men's characteristic styles may put women at a disadvantage in the workplace. If one person is trying to minimize status differences, maintain an appearance that everyone is equal, and save face for the other, while another person is trying to maintain the one-up position and avoid being positioned as one down, the person seeking the one-up position is likely to get it. At the same time, the person who has not been expending any effort to avoid the one-down position is likely to end up in it. Because women are more likely to take (or accept) the role of advice seeker, men are more inclined to interpret a ritual question from a woman as a request for advice.

## Ritual opposition

Apologizing, mitigating criticism with praise, and exchanging compliments are rituals common among women that men often take literally. A ritual common among men that women often take literally is ritual opposition.

A woman in communications told me she watched with distaste and distress as her office mate argued heatedly with another colleague about whose division should suffer budget cuts. She was even more surprised, however, that a short time later they were as friendly as ever. "How can you pretend that fight never happened?" she asked. "Who's pretending it never happened?" he responded, as puzzled by her question as she had been by his behavior. "It happened," he said, "and it's over." What she took as literal fighting to him was a routine part of daily negotiation: a ritual fight.

Many Americans expect the discussion of ideas to be a ritual fight—that is, an exploration through verbal opposition. They present their own ideas in the most certain and absolute form they can, and wait to see if they are challenged. Being forced to defend an idea provides an opportunity to test it. In the same spirit, they may play devil's advocate in challenging their colleagues' ideas—trying to poke holes and find weaknesses—as a way of helping them explore and test their ideas.

This style can work well if everyone shares it, but those unaccustomed to it are likely to miss its ritual nature. They may give up an idea that is challenged, taking the objections as an indication that the idea was a poor one. Worse, they may take the opposition as a personal attack and may find it impossible to do their best in a contentious environment. People unaccustomed to this style may hedge when stating their ideas in order to fend off potential attacks. Ironically, this posture makes their arguments appear weak and is more likely to invite attack from pugnacious colleagues than to fend it off.

Ritual opposition can even play a role in who gets hired. Some consulting firms that recruit graduates from the top business schools use a confrontational interviewing technique. They challenge the candidate to "crack a case" in real time. A partner at one firm told me, "Women tend to do less well in this kind of interaction, and it certainly affects who gets hired. But, in fact, many women who don't 'test well' turn out to be good consultants. They're often smarter than some of the men who looked like analytic powerhouses under pressure."

The level of verbal opposition varies from one company's culture to the next, but I saw instances of it in all the organizations I studied. Anyone who is uncomfortable with this linguistic style—and that includes some men as well as many women—risks appearing insecure about his or her ideas.

## Negotiating authority

In organizations, formal authority comes from the position one holds. But actual authority has to be negotiated day to day. The effectiveness of individual managers depends in part on their skill in negotiating authority and on whether others reinforce or undercut their efforts. The way linguistic style reflects status plays a subtle role in placing individuals within a hierarchy.

## *Managing up and down*

In all the companies I researched, I heard from women who knew they were doing a superior job and knew that their coworkers (and sometimes their immediate bosses) knew it as well, but believed that the higher-ups did not. They frequently told me that something outside themselves was holding them back and found it frustrating because they thought that all that should be necessary for success was to do a great job, that superior performance should be recognized and rewarded. In contrast, men often told me that if women weren't promoted, it was because they simply weren't up to snuff. Looking around, however, I saw evidence that men more often than women behaved in ways likely to get them recognized by those with the power to determine their advancement.

In all the companies I visited, I observed what happened at lunchtime. I saw young men who regularly ate lunch with their boss, and senior men who ate with the big boss. I noticed far fewer women who sought out the highest-level person they could eat with. But one is more likely to get recognition for work done if one talks about it to those higher up, and it is easier to do so if the lines of communication are already open. Furthermore, given the opportunity for a conversation with superiors, men and women are likely to have different ways of talking about their accomplishments because of the different ways in which they were socialized as children. Boys are rewarded by their peers if they talk up their achievements, whereas girls are rewarded if they play theirs down. Linguistic styles common among men may tend to give them some advantages when it comes to managing up.

All speakers are aware of the status of the person they are talking to and adjust accordingly. Everyone speaks differently when talking to a boss than when talking to a subordinate. But, surprisingly, the ways in which they adjust their talk may be different and thus may project different images of themselves.

Communications researchers Karen Tracy and Eric Eisenberg studied how relative status affects the way people give criticism. They devised a business letter that contained some errors and asked 13 male and 11 female college students to role-play delivering criticism under two scenarios. In the first, the speaker was a boss talking to a subordinate; in the second, the speaker was a subordinate talking to his or her boss. The researchers measured how hard the speakers tried to avoid hurting the feelings of the person they were criticizing.

One might expect people to be more careful about how they deliver criticism when they are in a subordinate position. Tracy and Eisenberg found that hypothesis to be true for the men in their study but not for the women. As they reported in *Research on Language and Social Interaction*, the women showed more concern about the other person's feelings when they were playing the role of superior.[3] In other words, the women were more careful to save face for the other person when they were managing down than when they were managing up. This pattern recalls the way girls are socialized: Those who are in some way superior are expected to downplay rather than flaunt their superiority.

In my own recordings of workplace communication, I observed women talking in similar ways. For example, when a manager had to correct a mistake made by her secretary, she did so by acknowledging that there were mitigating circumstances. She said, laughing, "You know, it's hard to do things around here, isn't it, with all these people coming in!" The manager was saving face for her subordinate, just like the female students role-playing in the Tracy and Eisenberg study.

Is this an effective way to communicate? One must ask, effective for what? The manager in question established a positive environment in her group, and the work was done effectively. On the other hand, numerous women in many different fields told me that their bosses say they don't project the proper authority.

## Indirectness

Another linguistic signal that varies with power and status is indirectness—the tendency to say what we mean without spelling it out in so many words. Despite the widespread belief in the United States that it's always best to say exactly what we mean, indirectness is a fundamental and pervasive element in human communication. It also is one of the elements that vary most from one culture to another, and it can cause enormous misunderstanding when speakers have different habits and expectations about how it is used. It's often said that American women are more indirect than American men, but in fact everyone tends to be indirect in some situations and in different ways. Allowing for cultural, ethnic, regional, and individual differences, women are especially likely to be indirect when it comes to telling others what to do, which is not surprising, considering girls' readiness to brand other girls as bossy. On the other hand, men are especially likely to be indirect when it comes to admitting fault or weakness, which also is not surprising, considering boys' readiness to push around boys who assume the one-down position.

At first glance, it would seem that only the powerful can get away with bald commands such as, "Have that report on my desk by noon." But power in an organization also can lead to requests so indirect that they don't sound like requests at all. A boss who says, "Do we have the sales data by product line for each region?" would be surprised and frustrated if a subordinate responded, "We probably do" rather than "I'll get it for you." Examples such as these notwithstanding, many researchers have claimed that those in subordinate positions are more likely to speak indirectly, and that is surely accurate in some situations. For example, linguist Charlotte Linde examined the black-box conversations that took place between pilots and copilots before airplane crashes.[4] In one particularly tragic instance, an Air Florida plane crashed into the Potomac River immediately after attempting takeoff from National Airport in Washington, D.C., killing all but 5 of the 74 people on board. The pilot, it turned out, had little experience flying in icy weather. The copilot had a bit more, and it became heartbreakingly clear on analysis that he had tried to warn the pilot but had done so indirectly. Alerted by Linde's observation, I examined the transcript of the conversations and found evidence of her hypothesis. The copilot repeatedly called attention to the bad weather and to ice buildup on other planes:

*Copilot:* Look how the ice is just hanging on his, ah, back, back there, see that? See all those icicles on the back there and everything?

*Pilot:* Yeah.

*[The copilot also expressed concern about the long waiting time since deicing.]*

*Copilot:* Boy, this is a, this is a losing battle here on trying to deice those things; it [gives] you a false feeling of security, that's all that does.
*[Just before they took off, the copilot expressed another concern—about abnormal instrument readings—but again he didn't press the matter when it wasn't picked up by the pilot.]*

*Copilot:* That don't seem right, does it? [3-second pause]. Ah, that's not right. Well—

*Pilot:* Yes it is, there's 80.

*Copilot:* Naw, I don't think that's right. [7-second pause] Ah, maybe it is.

Shortly thereafter, the plane took off, with tragic results. In other instances, as well as this one, Linde observed that copilots, who are second in command, are more likely to express themselves indirectly or otherwise mitigate, or soften, their communication when they are suggesting courses of action to the pilot. In an effort to avert similar disasters, some airlines now offer training for copilots to express themselves in more assertive ways.

This solution seems self-evidently appropriate to most Americans. But when I assigned Linde's article in a graduate seminar I taught, a Japanese student pointed out that it would be just as effective to train pilots to pick up on hints. This approach reflects assumptions about communication that typify Japanese culture, which places great value on the ability of people to understand one another without putting everything into words. Either directness or indirectness can be a successful means of communication as long as the linguistic style is understood by the participants.

In the world of work, however, there is more at stake than whether the communication is understood.

People in powerful positions are likely to reward styles similar to their own, because we all tend to take as self-evident the logic of our own styles. Accordingly, there is evidence that in the U.S. workplace, where instructions from a superior are expected to be voiced in a relatively direct manner, those who tend to be indirect when telling subordinates what to do may be perceived as lacking in confidence.

Consider the case of the manager at a national magazine who was responsible for giving assignments to reporters. She tended to phrase her assignments as questions. For example, she asked, "How would you like to do the X project with Y?" or said, "I was thinking of putting you on the X project. Is that okay?" This worked extremely well with her staff; they liked working for her, and the work got done in an efficient and orderly manner. But when she had her midyear evaluation with her own boss, he criticized her for not assuming the proper demeanor with her staff.

In any work environment, the higher-ranking person has the power to enforce his or her view of appropriate demeanor, created in part by linguistic style. In most U.S. contexts, that view is likely to assume that the person in authority has the right to be relatively direct rather than to mitigate orders. There also are cases, however, in which the higher-ranking person assumes a more indirect style. The owner of a retail operation told her subordinate, a store manager, to do something. He said he would do it, but a week later he still hadn't. They were able to trace the difficulty to the following conversation: She had said, "The bookkeeper needs help with the billing. How would you feel about helping her out?" He had said, "Fine." This conversation had seemed to be clear and flawless at the time, but it turned out that they had interpreted this simple exchange in very different ways. She thought he meant, "Fine, I'll help the bookkeeper out." He thought he meant, "Fine, I'll think about how I would feel about helping the bookkeeper out." He did think about it and came to the conclusion that he had more important things to do and couldn't spare the time.

To the owner, "How would you feel about helping the bookkeeper out?" was an obviously appropriate way to give the order "Help the bookkeeper out with the billing." Those who expect orders to be given as bald imperatives may find such locutions annoying or even misleading. But those for whom this style is natural do not think they are being indirect. They believe they are being clear in a polite or respectful way.

What is atypical in this example is that the person with the more indirect style was the boss, so the store manager was motivated to adapt to her style. She still gives orders the same way, but the store manager now understands how she means what she says. It's more common in U.S. business contexts for the highest-ranking people to take a more direct style, with the result that many women in authority risk being judged by their superiors as lacking the appropriate demeanor—and, consequently, lacking confidence.

## What to do?

I am often asked, What is the best way to give criticism? or What is the best way to give orders?—in other words, What is the best way to communicate? The answer is that there is no one best way. The results of a given way of speaking will vary depending on the situation, the culture of the company, the relative rank of speakers, their linguistic styles, and how those styles interact with one another. Because of all those influences, any way of speaking could be perfect for communicating with one person in one situation and disastrous with someone else in another. The critical skill for managers is to become aware of the workings and power of linguistic style, to make sure that people with something valuable to contribute get heard.

It may seem, for example, that running a meeting in an unstructured way gives equal opportunity to all. But awareness of the differences in conversational style makes it easy to see the potential for unequal access. Those who are comfortable speaking up in groups, who need little or no silence before raising their hands, or who speak out easily without waiting to be recognized are far more likely to get heard at meetings. Those who refrain from talking until it's clear that the previous speaker is finished, who wait to be recognized, and who are inclined to link their comments to those of others will do fine at a meeting where everyone else is following the same rules but will have a hard time getting heard in a meeting with people whose styles are more like the first pattern. Given the socialization typical of boys and girls, men are more likely to have learned the first style and women the second, making meetings more congenial for men than for women. It's common to observe women who participate actively in one-on-one discussions or in all-female groups but who are seldom heard in meetings with a large proportion of men. On the other hand, there are women who share the style more common among men, and they run a different risk—of being seen as too aggressive.

A manager aware of those dynamics might devise any number of ways of ensuring that everyone's ideas are heard and credited. Although no single solution will fit all contexts, managers who understand the dynamics of linguistic style can develop more adaptive and flexible approaches to running or participating in meetings, mentoring or advancing the careers of others, evaluating performance, and so on. Talk is the lifeblood of managerial work, and understanding that different people have different ways of saying what they mean will make it possible to take advantage of the talents of people with a broad range of linguistic styles. As the workplace becomes more culturally diverse and business becomes more global, managers will need to become even better at reading interactions and more flexible in adjusting their own styles to the people with whom they interact.

DEBORAH TANNEN is University Professor and a professor of linguistics at Georgetown University in Washington, D.C. She is the author of 15 books, including *You Just Don't Understand: Women and Men in Conversation* (William Morrow, 1990), which introduced to the general public the idea of female and male styles of communication. The material in this article is drawn from *Talking from 9 to 5* (Avon Books, 1995).

## Notes

1. L. Heatherington et al., "Two Investigations of 'Female Modesty' in Achievement Situations," *Sex Roles* 29, no. 11 (1993): 739–754.
2. J. Holmes, "Compliments and Compliment Responses in New Zealand English," *Anthropological Linguistics* 28, no. 4 (1986): 485–508.
3. K. Tracy and E. Eisenberg, "Giving Criticism: A Multiple Goals Case Study," *Research and Social Interaction* 24, no. 1 (1990/1991): 37–70.

4. C. Linde, "The Quantitative Study of Communicative Success: Politeness and Accidents in Aviation Discourse," *Language in Society* 17, no. 3 (1988): 375–399.

Reprinted from *Harvard Business Review*,
September–October 1995 (product #95510).

# 6

# Too Much Charisma Can Make Leaders Look Less Effective

By Jasmine Vergauwe, Bart Wille, Joeri Hofmans, Robert B. Kaiser, and Filip de Fruyt

Conventional wisdom suggests that the most charismatic leaders are also the best leaders. Charismatic leaders have, for instance, the ability to inspire others toward higher levels of performance and to instill deep levels of commitment, trust, and satisfaction. As a result, they are generally perceived by their subordinates to be more effective, compared with less charismatic leaders.[1]

But our research shows that while having at least a moderate level of charisma is important, having too much may hinder a leader's effectiveness. We conducted three studies, involving 800 business leaders globally and around 7,500 of their superiors, peers, and subordinates. Leaders occupied different managerial levels, ranging from supervisors to general managers. Our paper is forthcoming in the *Journal of Personality and Social Psychology*.

First, it's important to understand what charisma is. Traditional models of charismatic leadership state that charisma is not a personality trait, but simply exists in the eye of the beholder. In other words, charisma is *attributed to* someone, as opposed to being grounded in one's personality.[2]

However, the observation that people tend to agree in their perceptions of others' charisma levels suggests that it is not only a matter of attribution, and that this agreement might result from a personality-based foundation underlying these perceptions.[3] So the first goal of our research was to establish a measure of *charismatic personality*.

We gave leaders the Hogan Development Survey (HDS), a personality inventory specifically designed for work applications, and looked at how they scored on four personality tendencies: bold, colorful, mischievous, and imaginative. More-charismatic leaders score high on these traits, which is reflected in their high self-confidence, dramatic flair, readiness to test the limits, and expansive visionary thinking.

Next, we conducted a study to confirm this cluster of traits as a valid measure of charismatic personality. Using a sample of 204 business leaders, we showed that charismatic personality related to subordinates' perceptions of charismatic leadership. So leaders with a highly charismatic personality, as measured with HDS charisma, were also perceived to be highly charismatic by their subordinates. Using an archival data set from 1998 on a sample of 156 people, we further showed that HDS charisma levels could be predicted by people's charismatic behaviors (for example, being energetic, assertive, and generating enthusiasm).[4]

Our second goal was to investigate the relationship between charismatic personality and leader effectiveness. In a second study, 306 leaders (65% of them men) provided HDS self-ratings of their charismatic personality, while their coworkers provided ratings of their overall effectiveness using a 10-point rating scale, where 5 is *adequate* and 10 is *outstanding*. Taken together, 4,345 of their coworkers participated in this study: 666 superiors; 1,659 peers; and 2,020 subordinates. An average of 14 people rated each leader in terms of overall effectiveness.

Consistent with our expectations, we found that as charisma increased, so did perceived effectiveness— but only up to a certain point. As charisma scores continued to increase beyond the 60th percentile, which is just above the average score relative to the general population of working adults, perceived effectiveness started to decline. This trend was consistent across the three observer groups (subordinates, peers, and supervisors).

We also asked the leaders to evaluate their own effectiveness. As shown later, the more charismatic the leaders were, the higher they rated their own effectiveness. This discrepancy between self-perceptions and observer ratings is in line with other research demonstrating that leaders with high self-esteem typically overrate their performance on a variety of criteria.[5]

In a third study, we tested whether the effects of charismatic personality on effectiveness could be explained by looking at specific leader behaviors. To test this, we asked 287 business leaders (81% men) to rate their charismatic personality, and an average of 11 coworkers—including supervisors, peers, and subordinates—to rate each leader in terms of overall effectiveness. Additionally, coworkers now also rated leaders on two pairs of opposing leader-behavior dimensions: the extent to which they were *forceful* and *enabling* (tapping into the interpersonal behavior dimensions, or *how* they led), and the extent to which they were *strategic* and *operational* (representing the organizational dimensions, or *what* they led).

Although we did not find significant relationships between charisma and the interpersonal behavior dimensions, we found that highly charismatic leaders were perceived to engage in more strategic behavior and less operational behavior. But how can this explain lower effectiveness ratings for the most charismatic?

One explanation is that the costs associated with the desired trait (charisma) eventually come to outweigh its benefits. For highly charismatic leaders, we expected that the costs associated with a lack of operational behavior would come to outweigh the benefits delivered by strategic behavior when a certain level of charisma is exceeded. And that's exactly what we found: Highly charismatic leaders may be strategically ambitious, but this comes at the expense of getting day-to-day work activities executed in a proper manner, which can hurt perceived effectiveness. They failed, for example, in managing the day-to-day operations needed to implement their big strategic vision and in taking a methodical approach to getting things done in the near term. Further analysis showed that for leaders with lower levels of charisma, the opposite was true: They were found to be less effective because they lacked strategic behavior. For example, they did not spend enough time on long-term planning, and failed in taking a big-picture perspective, questioning the status quo, and encouraging innovation.

In terms of practical implications, our findings suggest that leaders should be aware of the potential drawbacks of being highly charismatic. Although it's difficult to draw a precise line between "just enough" and "too much" charisma, these are a few traits to look out for that can influence one's effectiveness. Self-confidence, for instance, may turn into overconfidence and narcissism in highly charismatic leaders, while risk tolerance and persuasiveness may start to translate into manipulative behavior. Further, the enthusiastic and entertaining nature of charisma may turn into attention-seeking behaviors that distract the organization from its mission, and extreme creativity may make highly charismatic leaders think and act in fanciful, eccentric ways.

For those whose charisma may be above optimal, coaching and development programs aimed at managing potential operational weaknesses, enhancing self-awareness, and improving self-regulation can be useful. Highly charismatic leaders would also benefit from receiving feedback from their coworkers on their effectiveness. That way, any gap between their perception and the perceptions of others will become clear. In contrast, coaching programs for leaders low on charisma might focus more on boosting their strategic behavior.

In sum, we found support for the idea that a leader can be too charismatic. Our findings suggest that highly charismatic leaders are perceived to be less effective, not for interpersonal reasons like self-centeredness but for business-related reasons that specifically relate to a lack of operational leader behavior.

We do want to point out that we didn't include situational factors in our study, which could influence the strength and shape of the relationship between leader charisma and effectiveness. Under certain conditions, such as in low-stress situations, this relationship may be strictly linear ("the more charisma the better"). However, we believe that high-stress and high-pressure situations are rather typical for a "normal" leadership context, enhancing the likelihood of finding a too-much-of-a-good-thing effect.[6] Additional studies will be important to further investigate the specific conditions under which charisma is desirable or not.

JASMINE VERGAUWE is a PhD candidate at the Department of Developmental, Personality, and Social Psychology, Ghent University. Her research interests include general and maladaptive personality traits, personality assessment, and leadership, with particular emphasis on traits as predictors of managerial performance and derailment. BART WILLE is assistant professor at the Department of Training and Education Sciences, University of Antwerp. His research focuses on professional development, strategic human resource development, career management and unfolding, and person-environment fit. JOERI HOFMANS is associate professor at the Research Group of Work and Organizational Psychology, Vrije Universiteit Brussel. His research interests include personality, emotions, and motivation at work, with particular emphasis on temporal dynamics. ROBERT B. KAISER is the president of Kaiser Leadership Solutions, based in Greensboro, N.C. His latest book, with coauthor Robert E. Kaplan, is *Fear Your Strengths: What You Are Best At Could Be Your Biggest Problem* (Berrett-Koehler, 2013). Find him online at kaiserleadership.com. FILIP DE FRUYT is senior full professor at the Department of Developmental, Personality, and Social Psychology, Ghent University. His research spans adaptive and maladaptive traits, their structure and development, cross-cultural manifestations of personality, and applied personality psychology.

## Notes

1. B. Shamir, R. J. House, and M. B. Arthur, "The Motivational Effects of Charismatic Leadership: A Self-Concept Based Theory," *Organization Science* 4, no. 4 (1993); T. Dvir et al., "Impact of Transformational Leadership on Follower Development and Performance: A Field Experiment," *Academy of Management Journal* 45, no. 4 (2002): 735–744; and J. A. Conger, R. N. Kanungo., and S. T. Menon, "Charismatic Leadership and Follower Effects," *Journal of Organizational Behavior* 21 (2000): 747–767.

2. Conger et al., "Charismatic Leadership and Follower Effects."

3. J. J. Sosik, "Self-Other Agreement on Charismatic Leadership," *Group and Organization Management* 26, no. 4 (2001).

4. L. R. Goldberg, "The Eugene-Springfield Community Sample." *ORI Technical Report* 48, no. 1 (2008).

5. T. A. Judge, J. A. LePine, and B. L. Rich, "Loving Yourself Abundantly: Relationship of Narcissistic Personality to Self- and Other Perceptions of Workplace Deviance, Leadership and Task and Contextual Performance," *Journal of Applied Psychology* 91, no. 4 (2006): 762–776.

6. J. R. Pierce and H. Aguinis, "The Too-Much-of-a-Good-Thing Effect in Management." *Journal of Management* 39, no. 2 (2013).

Reprinted from hbr.org, originally published
September 26, 2017 (product #H03WYV).

# Index

Index

# Invaluable insights
## always at your fingertips

With an All-Access subscription to
*Harvard Business Review*, you'll get
so much more than a magazine.

**Exclusive online content and tools**
you can put to use today

**My Library**, your personal workspace for sharing,
saving, and organizing HBR.org articles and tools

**Unlimited access** to more than 4,000 articles in the
*Harvard Business Review* archive

**Subscribe today at hbr.org/subnow**

# The most important management ideas all in one place.

We hope you enjoyed this book from *Harvard Business Review*. For the best ideas HBR has to offer turn to HBR's 10 Must Reads Boxed Set. From books on leadership and strategy to managing yourself and others, this 6-book collection delivers articles on the most essential business topics to help you succeed.

## HBR's 10 Must Reads Series

The definitive collection of ideas and best practices on our most sought-after topics from the best minds in business.

- Change Management
- Collaboration
- Communication
- Emotional Intelligence
- Innovation
- Leadership
- Making Smart Decisions

- Managing Across Cultures
- Managing People
- Managing Yourself
- Strategic Marketing
- Strategy
- Teams
- The Essentials

hbr.org/mustreads

**Buy for your team, clients, or event.**
Visit hbr.org/bulksales for quantity discount rates.